Prodeepta Das was born in Cuttack, in eastern India. He is a freelance photographer and author whose pictures have been published in over 30 children's books. In 1991 *Inside India*, which he also wrote, won the Commonwealth Photographer's Award. Prodeepta's books for Frances Lincoln include *P is for Pakistan*, *Prita Goes to India*, *K is for Korea*, *We are Britain!*, *Geeta's Day*, *I is for India*, *J is for Jamaica*, *Kamal Goes to Trinidad*, *P is for Poland*, *T is for Turkey*, *S is for South Africa* – which received an award from the U.S. Library of Congress as the best children's book about Africa in the year of publication – *R is for Russia* and *B is for Bangladesh*.

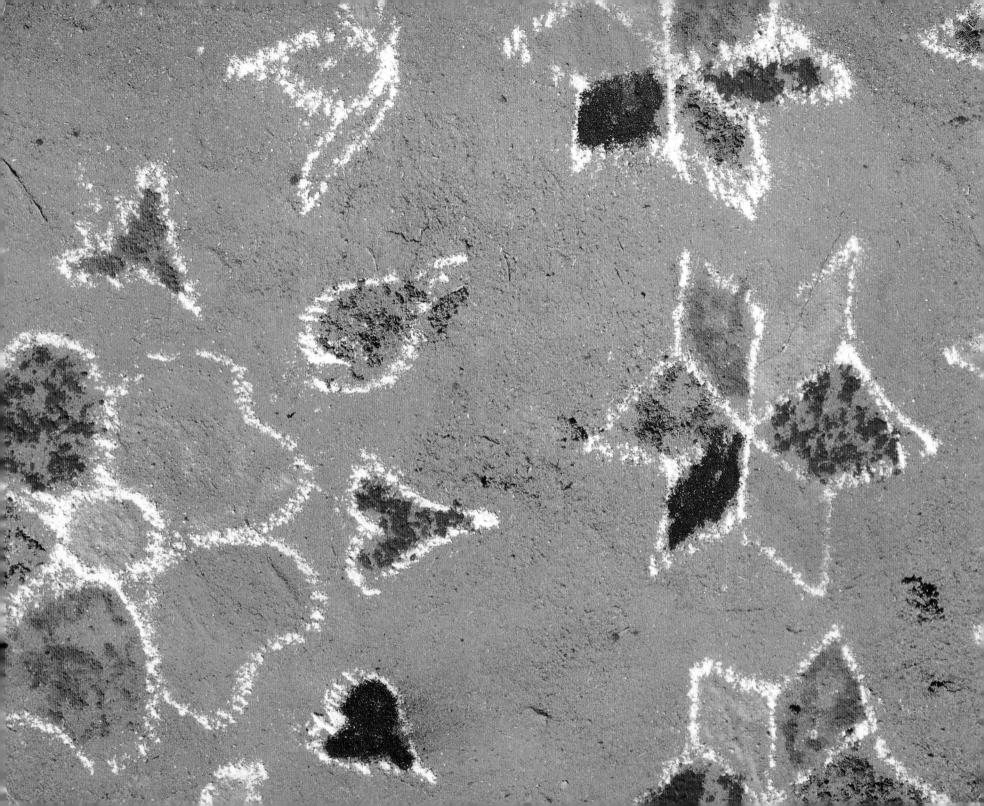

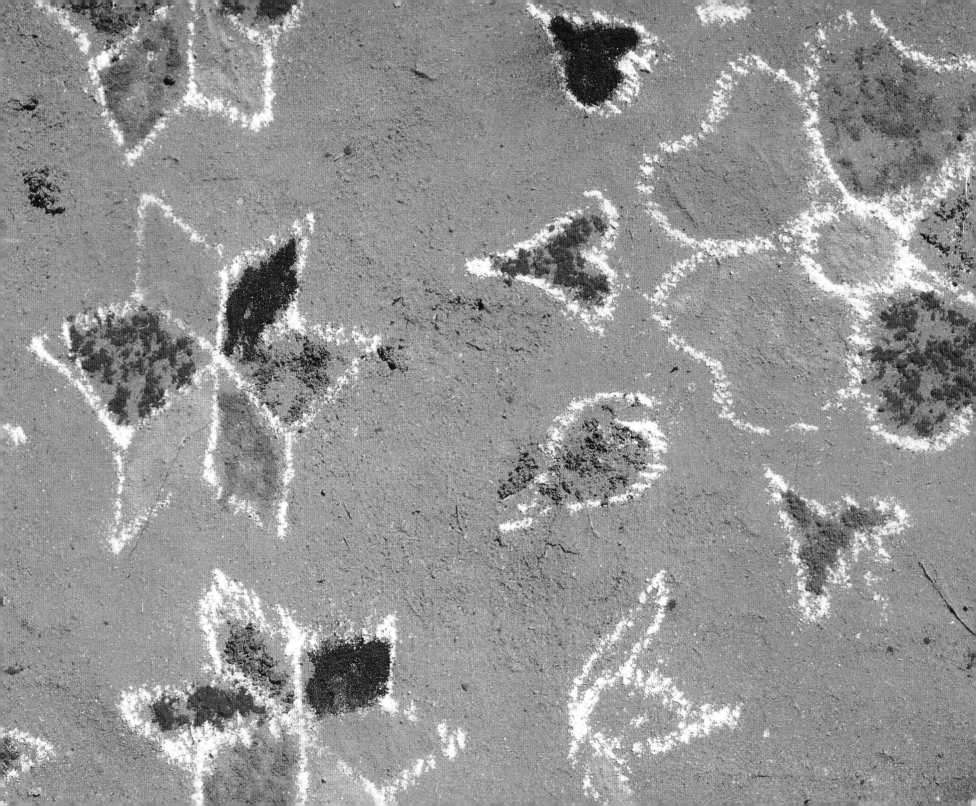

To Amrita, Prita, Shaun and Shauna for inspiring me,
and to Yvonne for support and advice.

First published in Great Britain in 1996 by
Frances Lincoln Children's Books,
74-77 White Lion Street, London, N1 9PF
www.franceslincoln.com

This updated paperback edition first published in 2016

A CIP catalogue record for this book is available from the British Library.

ISBN 978-1-84780-757-1

Printed in China

9 8 7 6 5 4 3 2 1

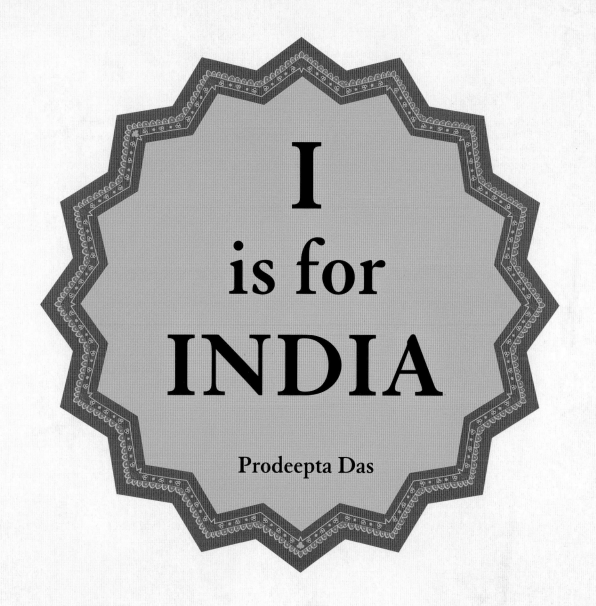

I
is for
INDIA

Prodeepta Das

Frances Lincoln
Children's Books

AUTHOR'S NOTE

India is a nation with a long, rich history, now a major developing country confidently embracing modern times.

It is full of surprising contrasts: vast open landscapes and small towns bursting at the seams; Hindus, Moslems, Sikhs, Christians and many other religions, often existing side by side, each with their own form of worship and way of life; quiet villages and sprawling cities where social changes take place at a dizzying rate. Nevertheless, some things are the same everywhere: the warmth of the people, their zest for life, and their fondness for rich colours.

I come from Odisha, in eastern India, and the words and images in this book reflect the India that I know and love. I hope they will inspire young people to go further and explore the colour, excitement and mystery of this great country.

Prodeepta

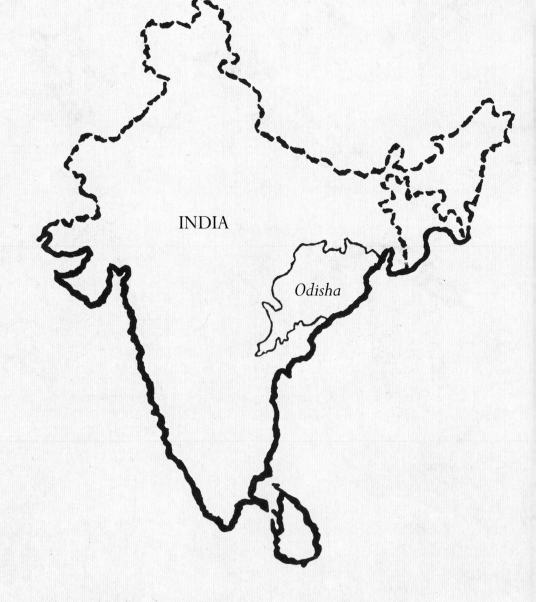

INDIA

Odisha

is for the Alphabet children learn at school. India has many languages, each with its own alphabet. These village schoolchildren are learning Odia, the alphabet of the state of Odisha. Their teacher writes out the first few letters on each child's slate, and then the children call out the letters as they go over them.

is for Bollywood. India makes the highest number of films in the world. Most are made in Mumbai and are known as Bollywood films. They use songs and dances and well-known actors to draw people to the cinemas. Seeing a film in a multi-screen cinema in a modern shopping centre is a family outing children look forward to.

is for Carrom, a very popular board game in India. The black-and-cream pieces are placed around the red Queen on the board. By flicking the plastic striker, the players try to hit as many of their pieces into the four corner holes as possible. The Queen carries the highest number of points. Players often argue about how and where to place the striker and how to strike!

is for Diwali, the Festival of Lights – a celebration of the Hindu god Rama returning home to his kingdom after fourteen years' exile. Between mid-October and mid-November, houses glow with earthen lamps on verandahs, rooftops, walls and windowsills. Children wear new clothes for the festival, and families gather to let off fireworks.

Ee

is for Elephant, an animal feared by all other jungle creatures. Elephants in India have smaller eyes and teeth than elephants in Africa. Tamed elephants have always been used to carry people and heavy goods. Now, as the forests disappear and people are using trucks more and more, national parks provide elephants with safe places to live.

Ff is for Family and Family life, which is very strong in India. In the villages, members of several generations live under the same roof, but in crowded cities this is not always possible. More and more people are choosing to have smaller families. Children learn when very young to respect their elders, who have special places in the families.

G g is for Gold, which people love to buy and wear. When an Indian girl is small, she has her ears pierced and wears gold studs. Later, when she marries, she is given gold and silver jewellery by her relatives and wears much of it for her wedding.

Hh is for Haat or markets, which are held in the open air or in covered stalls. People come to buy and sell fruit, vegetables, grain, spices, clothes and many other things. Though more and more malls are being built, Haat are still popular. Haat are cheap, colourful and extremely noisy places!

I i

is for India, a vast country with a population of over a billion. India's people speak more than 22 different languages, follow many different religions, and live in every kind of landscape – from hot deserts and plains to cold, mountainous areas – but everyone is warm and friendly and proud to be Indian.

is for Jilabi, a mouthwatering, crunchy yellow sweet. To make it, the sweet-maker presses chickpea-flour batter through a mould into a deep pan of boiling oil to fry, until it looks like a fat spider's web. Then after a dipping in sugar syrup, it is ready to eat.

is for Kameez, a loose tunic that women and girls all over India like to wear. The tunics are made in many different styles and in every colour imaginable. Some are hand-woven and decorated with beautiful embroidery.

is for Lassi, a refreshing yoghurt drink made from cow's or goat's milk. Seasoned with salt and pepper, it is cooling and soothing, but it tastes equally delicious sweetened with nuts and spices.

is for Mehndi, a tattoo-like decoration often worn by young women at weddings and festivals. The beautician grinds henna leaves with oil, making a green paste. Then she squeezes the paste through a cone to make patterns on the customer's hands and feet. As a design dries, it turns bright red. It can be washed off later with water.

is for Namaskar or Namaste – hands folded and held up in greeting. It is our way of saying, "I respect you."

is for Odissi, an ancient traditional dance. In the past, the odissi was only performed in temples by men and women wearing special silk saris, crowns, and ankle bells. Now it can take place anywhere. It is one of the four most important Indian classical dances and, like ballet, takes many years of training to perform it well.

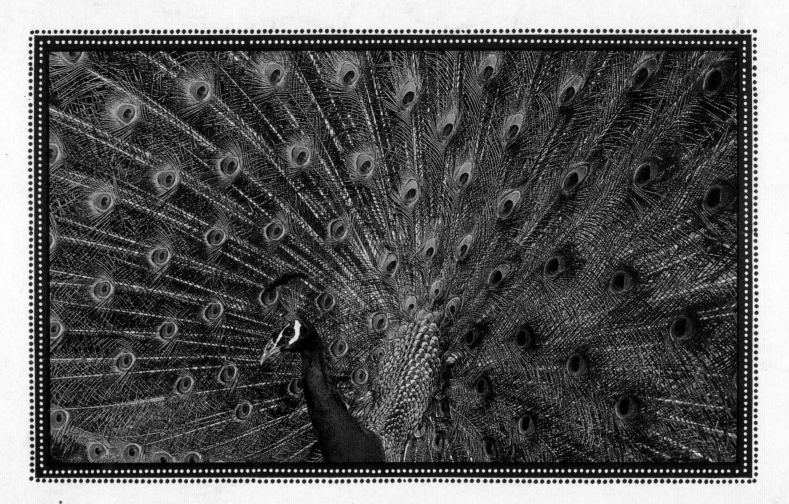

is for Peacock, India's national bird. People believe that peacocks come out to dance when it is going to rain. The birds spread out their beautiful plumes like a fan when they are courting, just before the monsoon season begins.

is for the Quran or Koran, the book
of the prophet Mohammed which
Muslim children learn from when
they are very young. They sit on
prayer mats facing in the direction of
the holy city of Mecca and read aloud
from the pages of the Quran, which
is printed in beautiful Arabic letters.

 is for Rice, which is eaten boiled, fried or made into cakes or puddings. The rice is planted when the rains come. Once the young green plants have turned a rich golden brown, families work together cutting, threshing and winnowing the grain. Rice is everywhere: it is used during religious ceremonies, at weddings; coloured rice powder even decorates the walls and floors.

S s

is for Sadhu or holy man.
You can tell a sadhu by his long
hair and beard, by the special
marks on his forehead, by his
necklace and his loincloth.
Sadhus have chosen to leave their
families and possessions to spend
all their time praying. People
respect their way of life and give
them food and drink. Some
sadhus stay in one place, but
others travel around, sleeping in
temples or outside – wherever
they happen to be.

is for Train. India has one of the largest railway networks in the world. Every day local trains carry millions of people to work in the cities; often they are so full that passengers sit on the roof! A special government programme offers people free train tickets every two to four years. This has encouraged travelling with family to explore new places.

is for Umbrella, used not only when it rains but also to give shade from the hot sun. The most beautiful umbrellas are made in the small village of Pipili in the state of Odisha.

is for Veena, an ancient Indian musical instrument with seven strings. It is made from a piece of jackfruit wood, with a hollow at the top end. The veena takes many years to learn to play.

W **w**

is for Water. In the rainy season
there is too much of it, and in
the dry season too little. Many
towns only receive piped water
for a few hours each day, so
everyone stores it in big
containers to have enough
for the rest of the day. In the
villages, people collect rain
water in tanks or sink deep
wells. People use the rivers,
canals and ponds for washing,
watering crops, and keeping
cattle clean. Ritual bathing
is done in the holy river at
Varanasi and in the sea at Puri.

is for Xmas, as Christmas is usually known in India. It is a time when Christian families gather together to celebrate. They decorate their houses and churches with stars and lights and receive presents from Father Xmas. In southern India, Xmas is celebrated in January.

is for Yatra, a religious fair often held in a temple. Pilgrims, holy men, and people of all ages come from near and far to worship, listen to songs of prayer, and watch shows based on stories from holy books. Sometimes, when a yatra goes on for a few days, people sleep outside in tents.

Zz is for the Zodiac, or *Greha*, of 12 birth signs in astrology. The zodiac is very important to the Indian people, whatever their religion. It is based on a 3,000 year old Sanskrit manuscript. When a baby is born, an astrologer, or *joytish*, is called in to work out the baby's birth sign. He makes calculations in chalk on the floor and writes them on a palm leaf with an iron pen. The leaf is then wrapped in a clean cloth and treasured by the parents together with their own hopes for the baby's future.

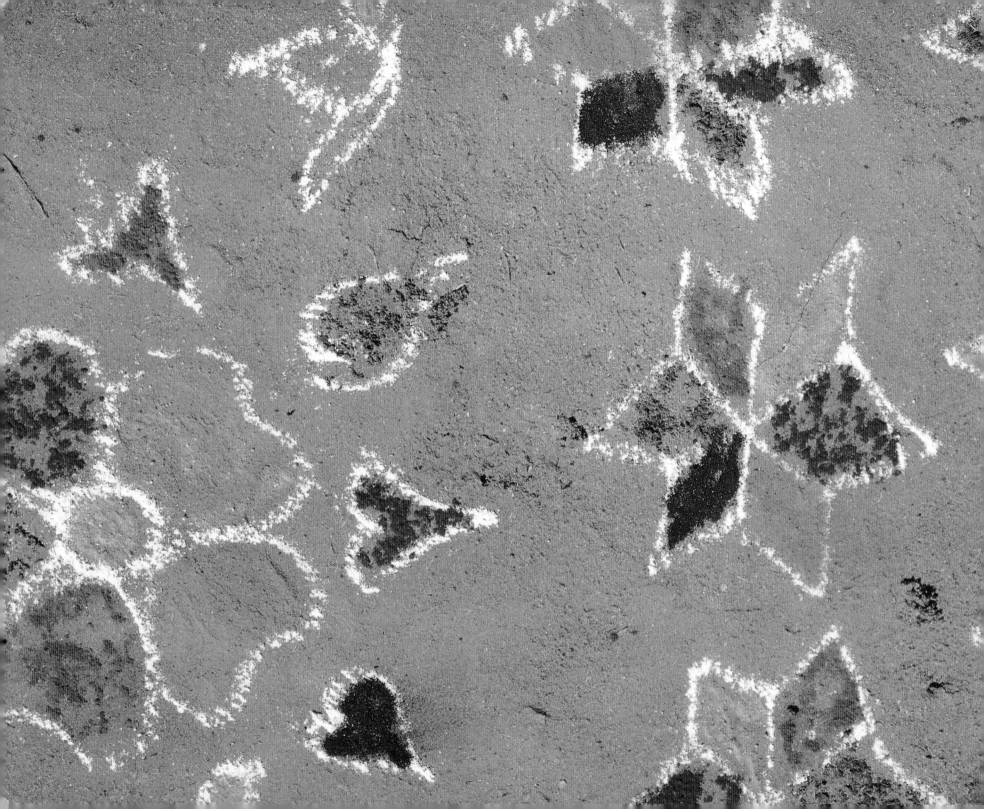

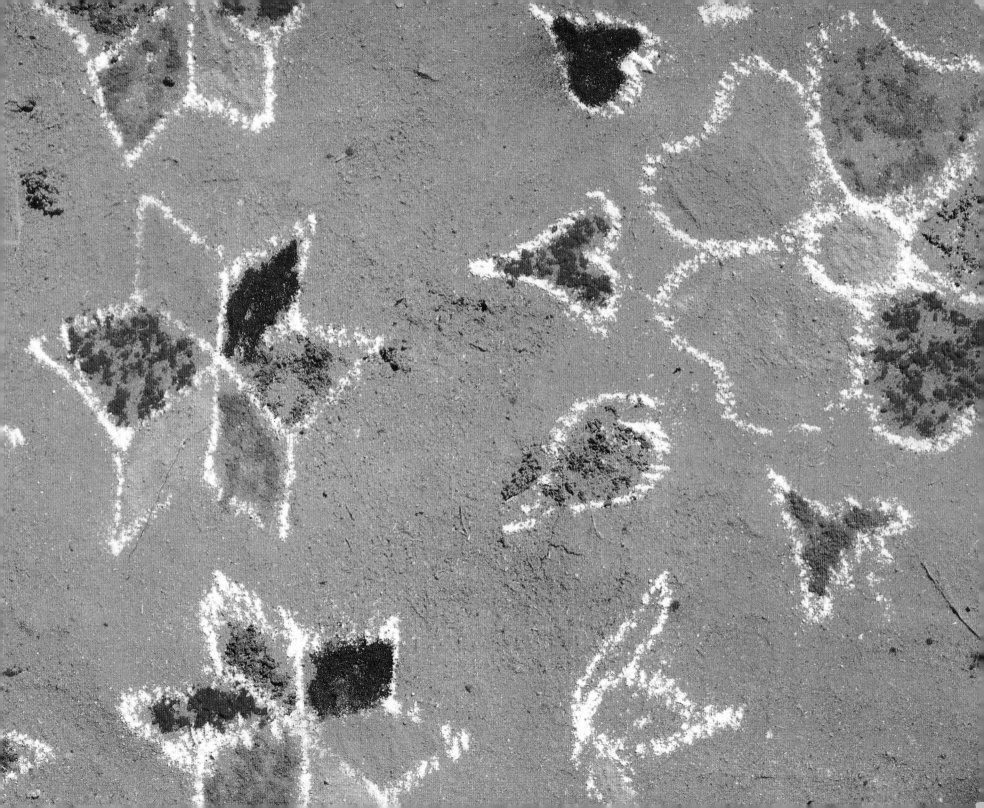

MORE TITLES IN THE WORLD ALPHABETS SERIES
PUBLISHED BY FRANCES LINCOLN CHILDREN'S BOOKS

J is for Jamaica
by Benjamin Zephaniah and Prodeepta Das
978-1-84507-609-2

From Cricket to Pumpkin, from Hummingbird to Yam – this is
a photographic alphabet showing Jamaica in all its colourful
diversity. In vibrant rhyming verse, Benjamin Zephaniah explores
some of the sights, sounds and tastes of Jamaica, from the bustling
capital of Kingston, to the peaceful and serene Blue Mountain.

P is for Pakistan
by Shazia Razzak and Prodeepta Das
978-1-84780-089-3

In this photographic alphabet, the author introduces young readers
to some of the customs, religions and cultures – both ancient and
modern – that make up this fast-developing country. Focusing on
both city and country life, this is a celebration of Pakistan in all its
aspects, from Dhobi to Jasmine, from Hijab to Water buffalo.

R is for Russia
by Vladimir Kabakov and Prodeepta Das
978-1-84780-427-3

From Dacha to Winter Palace, from Easter Eggs to Kremlin,
here is a photographic alphabet of everything that is best about
Russia. Over centuries of splendour, revolution and change, Russia
has produced some of the greatest scientists, sportsmen and
women, writers, dancers and composers in the world. The perfect
introduction to a fascinating country.

Frances Lincoln titles are available from all good bookshops.
You can also buy books and find out more about your favourite titles,
authors and illustrators on our website: www.franceslincoln.com